A BRIEF HISTORY: PACIFIC ENGINEERING AND PRODUCTION COMPANY OF NEVADA (PEPCON)

HENDERSON, NEVADA, 1955–1992

JOHN GIBSON
AND
DAVE THAYER

To order additional copies of this book, contact:
Xlibris
1-888-795-4274
www.Xlibris.com
Orders@Xlibris.com

Incorporation and A Mission to Produce Perchlorate Chemicals in the 1950s

Pacific Engineering and Production Company of Nevada (PEPCON) was incorporated in Henderson, Nevada, about seven miles southeast of Las Vegas, in November of 1955 by Edgar J. Marston (La Jolla, CA), Fred D. Gibson Sr. (Las Vegas, NV), and John V. Mueller (Reno, NV). Initially, PEPCON provided consulting services specializing in mining and chemical plant design. It was also the operator of a chlorine gas packaging plant (servicing area businesses that had swimming pools) and a sodium hypochlorite (household bleach) manufacturing operation using the brand name "Boulder White."

PEPCON's principal managers on its founding were Fred D. Gibson, Sr. and Fred D. Gibson, Jr. Both had worked previously at Western Electrochemical Company located several miles to the east of PEPCON. Fred D. Gibson Sr., who had a degree in mining engineering and training in other technical fields, was the General Manager. Western Electrochemical Company, originally located in Culver City, CA and then moved to Nevada, was within the Basic Magnesium, Inc. facility, which between 1942 and 1944 constituted the largest magnesium production plant in the world. Fred D. Gibson, Sr. was the first employee hired for that operation in order to lay out the plant, water, power, and waste facilities that were constructed quickly to support the urgent needs of the U.S. Government in World War II.

The work at Western Electrochemical Company by Fred D. Gibson, Jr. included development of an electrolytic process to produce manganese metal as well as work on other products including perchlorates. Potassium perchlorate was an oxidizer used in solid rocket motors (SRMs) but it produced a very visible, and therefore undesirable in the military context, trail in the sky. The U.S. Navy preferred the use of ammonium perchlorate, which does not produce such a visible trail. The challenge with ammonium perchlorate, however, was to identify an efficient manufacturing process, since at that time a solid platinum anode was required to produce the material and platinum was expensive and eroded quickly with no known way to recover it. Fred D. Gibson, Jr. worked on this issue and eventually identified a solution, that is, the use of a lead dioxide plated graphite anode.

In 1954, Western Electrochemical Company entered into negotiations with and was acquired by American Potash and Chemical Company. As a result, Fred D. Gibson, Sr. and Fred D. Gibson, Jr. left to found PEPCON; Fred D. Gibson, Jr. departed American Potash in May of 1956. Early work by PEPCON was performed in leased office, laboratory, and manufacturing facilities—including the locomotive house that fronted on a railroad line—from Stauffer Chemical in the Basic Magnesium Incorporated (BMI) complex. Emmitt Kleba was hired as a chemist and performed important research and development work related to optimization of electrolytic cells. Sodium hypochlorite (12-15% bleach) was manufactured at this time.

In the mid-1950s, Fred D. Gibson, Sr. purchased first 140 acres with a partner (Ken Walsh, president of Western Electrochemical Company), and then 600 acres of undeveloped land in Henderson to the northwest of Black Mountain. The 140 acres included parts of sections 9 and 16 where a key potable water well was located; the 600 acres were comprised of the southern and northern halves of sections 10 and 15 respectively.

The 600 acres were contributed to PEPCON by Mr. Gibson. Eventually, the 140 acre parcel was transferred to PEPCON. The PEPCON facility was built in 1958 on 13 acres within this 740 acre area two miles west of the BMI industrial complex.

In 1956, the natural gas company in the area requested and was granted permission to install a 16-inch diameter natural gas transmission line from east to west under the area where the PEPCON plant would later be built to serve Las Vegas' growing population. Gas service to the PEPCON plant was relatively minor, principally for use in boiler operations. The electric resistance welded (ERW) pipe of "limited service"[21] quality operated at approximately 300 psig.

PEPCON's primary mission was to produce perchlorate-based oxidizer chemicals, including sodium perchlorate and ammonium perchlorate (AP). AP was then, and still is, the preferred solid oxidizer, based on its performance characteristics (including lack of a trail as noted above), in multiple U.S. space and Department of Defense programs that require a solid rocket propellant for various propulsion systems. Moreover, AP's performance and burning characteristics have advantages over other oxidizers.

The original use of AP was in JATO (jet assist take-off) and RATO (rocket assist take-off) systems for military aircraft beginning in the 1940s. Primary programs included Minuteman, Polaris, Poseidon, MX, Titan (for which PEPCON was the sole supplier until it ended its operations), Delta, Atlas, Peacekeeper, Standard Missile, and, beginning in the early 1980s, the Space Shuttle. AP by itself is stable, not explosive, and will not burn. It does provide oxygen in formulations, such as in propellants, where the oxygen is used, sometimes under water or in the vacuum of space, in order to enhance controlled combustion for various purposes.

PEPCON's manufacturing process was energy intensive. In the Chlorate Building, an electrolytic process, requiring substantial electricity, was employed in cells on multiple circuits, which in the presence of water, converted salt (sodium chloride) to sodium chlorate and then to sodium perchlorate with some excess hydrogen gas, which was safely vented. Sodium perchlorate was then moved to another manufacturing location (Process Building/Batch House) and reacted with ammonium chloride, which was generated by reacting hydrochloric acid and ammonia on site, and heated to produce ammonium perchlorate in liquid slurry form. This material was then sent to the crystallizer tanks and cooled to crystallize the AP out of solution, leaving excess salt in solution (filtrate). The salt was separated and the AP was then dried in a rotary dryer as a last step or, if needed, dried in the batch dryer and then blended to achieve desired particle size distributions. Sodium perchlorate was primarily employed as the intermediate to manufacture AP but also sold in later years as a stand-alone product.

The key innovation developed by PEPCON in the late 1950s as a result of R&D that was partially funded by the U.S. Navy, and that was patented in 1960 by Fred D. Gibson, Jr. (patent number 2,945,791), was the efficient and reliable process of plating lead dioxide to a graphite anode substrate. This enabled production of perchlorates, principally ammonium perchlorate, at very high rates at a lower cost level than using the existing technology, which relied upon solid platinum anodes. Subsequently, the Department of Defense and its agencies and prime contractors requested and encouraged PEPCON to demonstrate the technology in a pilot plant.

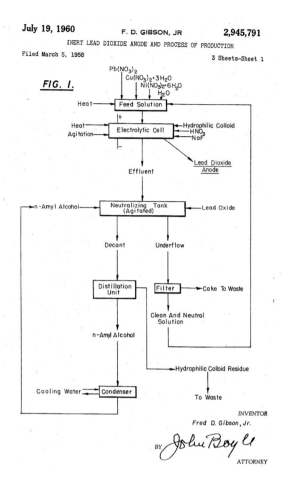

INVENTOR
Fred D. Gibson, Jr.

BY *John Boyle*

ATTORNEY

Early Ammonium Perchlorate Pilot Plant Operations

The pilot plant to manufacture AP at PEPCON was designed by Fred D. Gibson, Jr. and Bob Kesterson and built by them between August and December of 1958 to achieve a production rate of up to 2,000 pounds/day. The plant was located on Gibson Road, near Lake Mead Hwy/Route 146. In 1959, the annual AP production capacity was increased to 1.2 million pounds/year. The water used in the process was obtained from groundwater aquifers at the PEPCON plant. This was a critical resource for the isolated plant and although a few wells were used, the principle water source was located one mile west of the PEPCON plant in section 9 first drilled in 1941, which produced high quality and potable water.

Key employees and officers in the late 1950s – early 1960s, many of whom remained into the late 1980s, included: Fred D. Gibson, Sr. (1955-1966), Fred D. Gibson, Jr. (originally Plant Manager and later President and CEO of parent company American Pacific Corporation until the late 1990s and on the Board of Directors much longer), Tom War (VP and Secretary-Treasurer), James I. Gibson (joining in the early 1960s, (VP Engineering and eventually President in the 1980s)), Leroy (Roy) Westerfield (Controller, hired in 1960), Tom Harden (Chief Engineer), and Robert Thayer (Manager of the Anode Production Operation). Bruce Halker, who was hired in 1959, had worked at the Western Electrochemical Company in Henderson with Fred D. Gibson, Jr. He worked in the laboratory for many years before becoming Plant Manager and Vice President of Operations, which was his position to the end of PEPCON operations in Henderson.

PEPCON Plant Opening, Representatives of Thiokol, Jack Gibson, Fred D. Gibson, Sr. (3rd from left) and Fred D. Gibson, Jr (far right), 1962

Ribbon Cutting at PEPCON, L-R, John Mueller, Dr. Harold Ritchie (Thiokol CEO 1970-1973, later on the board of PEPCON), Fred D. Gibson, Jr. 1962

Further PEPCON expansion occurred in the 1961-62 period when four electrolytic circuits were put into operation for production of sodium chlorate and sodium perchlorate. A submerged combustion evaporation system, ammonium chloride reaction vessel, 30,000 gallon hydrochloric acid storage vessel, liquid ammonia tanks, crystallizer tanks, batch dryer, and other equipment enabled non-integrated AP production of up to 20 million pounds per year. The total cost to build the plant as it existed in 1962 was $3 million of which $2.4 million was borrowed from American Cyanamid. The $2.4 million debt was amended twice and resolved in 1968. Production of AP at the facility in 1963 was approximately 15 million pounds, which as it turned out, was the highest level achieved until the 1980s.

In the early 1960s, there were four U.S. producers of AP: PEPCON, American Potash (two miles to the east), Hooker-Foote, and Pennsalt (Pennwalt). Although 1963 was an excellent year for AP sales, because of policy decisions by the U.S. Government, there would be a declining market for AP in the 1964-1966 time frame, which led both Hooker-Foote and Pennsalt to exit the AP market. American Potash and then its successor as of 1967, Kerr McGee Chemical, remained the only U.S. competitor to PEPCON until the end of PEPCON operations in 1988.

Water Well Construction, circa 1958

PEPCON Plant Construction, 1958

From the inception of manufacturing activities, AP was recovered from the filtrate. In the early 1970s, however, a system was devised to decompose the AP by treatment with sodium hydroxide. This process resulted in ammonia, which was recovered by means of a hydrochloric acid scrubber. Recovered ammonium chloride was returned to the process. Filtrate containing sodium perchlorate was thereafter used in the front end of the process feeding electrolytic cells.

AP and the other perchlorate based chemicals produced at PEPCON, although very stable and nonflammable in pure form, could be hazardous if mixed with organic materials, flammable substances, or fuels. Therefore, precautions were taken in manufacturing processes, safety practices, and the repeated training of employees, to avoid contamination of the perchlorate based chemicals with flammable substances or fuels. PEPCON had comprehensive safety rules that were implemented and subjected to continuous revision and updating by the plant safety committee, which was comprised of management and hourly employees who met regularly.

PEPCON Plant, Henderson, NV 1965

In 1968, a new equipment business was added to manufacture sodium hypochlorite generators for use in water treatment/odor control at various locations around the world, including: power plants, water/sewage treatment plants, desalinization feed waters, and offshore oil drilling platforms. Sodium hypochlorite is also an oxidizing agent. In this process, compounds that cause undesirable odors are oxidized to innocuous substances, which results in elimination of the odors. Two other key employees joined the company in this time frame: Bob Ferraro, who was manager of customer relations for the equipment business for 30 years and Dr. Raymond Rhees (Ph.D., Chemistry), who was Vice President of Research for over 20 years.

Total revenue in 1968 was $560,000 and in 1969, $1,150,000, almost all attributable to AP. Beyond the equipment business, there was a major effort in 1969 to reduce the dependence of PEPCON on the sale of AP, which was an on-going effort over a long period of time.[1] The largest equipment business sale was a $5 million project in Saudi Arabia. A large engineering services project was for a Weyerhaeuser facility in Washington State that provided a means to diversity in an operation that had previously been producing only chlorine gas.

1970s: Going Public and Meeting Challenges

The company went public in February of 1970. The proceeds of that offering were used to retire debt, fund research and development programs, and to organize and then implement marketing programs.[2]

The early 1970s were challenging because of lower demand for AP. In 1971, sales volume of AP was high (over 10 million pounds); however, pricing was very low, which was problematic. PEPCON believed this was caused by several factors but principally the pricing policies of its competitor, which was the subject of litigation initiated in 1970. The situation was so dire that future participation in the AP market by PEPCON was in jeopardy. In 1971, new policies were employed by the U.S. Government that resulted in a commitment from key customer Thiokol for AP at prices higher than in 1971.

In March of 1970, after consultations by Fred D. Gibson, Jr. with U.S. Government representatives who assessed the relevant facts, PEPCON initiated a lawsuit in the U.S. District Court in Utah against American Potash and Chemical Company and its successor, Kerr McGee Chemical, seeking damages and injunctive relief under the anti-trust laws of the U.S. The matter was tried in May of 1973. A memorandum decision was handed down in February of 1974, which found in favor of PEPCON and against the defendants. The court found that the defendants had attempted to monopolize trade in the AP industry from 1966 to 1970 and had also engaged in unlawful price discrimination amongst customers. The damages phase was tried in March of 1975 and in February of 1976, the court awarded damages, including attorneys' fees in the amount of $5.1M.[5] C. Keith Rooker was the primary litigator for PEPCON in this matter. Mr. Rooker later joined the company as a senior executive extending to the late 1990's and as a Board member of American Pacific Corporation until 2014.

In March, 1972, the National Aeronautics and Space Administration (NASA) announced that it would employ a solid propellant booster for the future Space Shuttle program. The change in U.S. Government policies and, in addition, the forthcoming Space Shuttle program, which was then confirmed to use AP, led to the decision by PEPCON to continue to participate in the AP market.

The year 1973 was a low water mark for AP production at PEPCON (approximately 3.5 million pounds). The demand for AP was also low into 1974 and the AP plant at PEPCON was shut down for the first four months of 1975. PEPCON believed that the decline in AP sales was due to a reduction in demand for various military/defense related rockets and missiles in addition to the AP pricing practices of Kerr McGee Chemical. The AP that was manufactured in 1974 was limited mostly to high purity material, extremely low in alkali metal content, which was used in research and in certain missile programs.[3]

The development of NASA's Space Shuttle in the 1970s leading to the first launch in 1981 was critical for PEPCON. Each Space Shuttle had two solid rocket motors that contained, in the aggregate, approximately 1.6 million pounds of the oxidizer AP, which comprised 70%, by weight, of the propellant. The other 30% was comprised mostly of powdered aluminum and a polymer-binder material. PEPCON sold AP to Thiokol, based in Utah, for this purpose, with shipments beginning in 1979, and the propellant was manufactured into solid rocket motor sets at Thiokol facilities in northern Utah.

At the PEPCON plant, the AP manufactured was typically stored in either polypropylene or steel type containers in the plant, normally 55 gallon (about 550 pounds net AP) capacity. Many of the steel drums were U.S. Department of Transportation (DOT) approved for transportation of oxidizers and smaller quantities were shipped to customers in these containers or in smaller containers of 30 gallon capacity. The poly drums were not U.S. DOT approved for transportation on roads so these containers were used strictly in the plant for intermediate storage. Most of the AP product shipped to major higher volume customers was shipped in aluminum tote or econo bins that were either cylindrical or square, about 6 feet tall, and with net weight capacity of 4,500-5000 pounds each.

Between 1970 and 1975, the principal customers for PEPCON AP were Thiokol and UTC. In 1975, sales of dimensionally stable lead dioxide plated (on graphite substrate) anodes were higher. The outside sales of electrolytic cells (beyond internal use for manufacturing perchlorates) were for use in waste-water treatment and in home swimming pool chlorinators. The largest customer at this time was Gen-Chlor International.

In 1977, there was bad news for PEPCON in the American Potash/Kerr McGee anti-trust litigation. The defendants appealed the prior decisions and in February of 1977, the U.S. Court of Appeals for the Tenth Circuit reversed the judgment. PEPCON appealed this decision but to no avail. After the defendants filed counterclaims, both parties agreed to dismiss all claims against each other.[6]

In 1978, the primary customer for AP was UTC/Chemical Systems Division (over half of AP sales) and Thiokol (over 25% of AP sales).

1980-1987: PEPCON Acquired by American Pacific Corporation, Space Shuttle Activity

In 1980, sales of sodium perchlorate as an end product, principally for use in the mining industry became more prominent, although at low margins. A rehabilitation of the perchlorate chemical plant occurred in 1980. Also in 1980, the first static fire of a Space Shuttle Solid Rocket Motor using AP from PEPCON occurred at Thiokol facilities in Utah, which was a major milestone. Thereafter, in early 1981, the Space Shuttle Columbia made the first successful flight of the program utilizing the two solid rocket motors with AP as the primary component. This was a major development for PEPCON.

Beginning in the 1980s and progressing over a period of years, PEPCON provided engineering services and cells for a perchlorate chemicals plant located in Egypt, about 30 miles from Cairo. Replacement parts for this operation were an ongoing source of revenue.

1982: Acquisition by American Pacific Corporation

In April of 1982, all of the stock of PEPCON was acquired by American Pacific Corporation (AMPAC), a California based real estate investment trust. John E. Wertin, a principal at AMPAC, had previously held a large stock position in PEPCON. He was approached by the president of PEPCON, Fred D. Gibson, Jr., to consider possible collaboration. After the acquisition, the management structure changed but all of the principals at PEPCON remained in place as PEPCON operated as a subsidiary of AMPAC.

In 1983, a significant expansion occurred at the PEPCON Henderson facility increasing AP capacity to 32 million pounds per year. This included the addition of two additional full electrolytic cell lines to the core process of producing sodium perchlorate. Capital expenses in 1983 were $5.3 million, $3 million of that being for plant expansion. An office upgrade at the PEPCON plant was made during this time.

During 1983-1984, more than 80% of chemical sales were to Morton Thiokol Inc. (Utah). As of 1984, there were 21 buildings and 87,500 square feet "under roof" at the PEPCON facility.[11]

1985: Divesture of Non-Nevada Real Estate Holdings

In September of 1985, due to liquidity challenges, a divesture was completed wherein AMPAC exchanged with principal stockholder John E. Wertin real estate assets in California, New York, and Florida along with other assets for shares of stock, which were thereupon retired. The structure of AMPAC, a Delaware corporation publicly traded on the NASDAQ exchange, thereafter became the AMPAC non-operating parent company with only two subsidiaries: PEPCON (for chemical manufacturing) and Ampac Development Company (for developing the land surrounding the PEPCON plant). The business operations became: 1. Chemical manufacturing (perchlorates); 2. Water pollution and abatement equipment manufacturing; and 3. Industrial real estate development. Ampac Development Company's focus was to develop the approximately 460 acres of real estate in the area surrounding the PEPCON plant site called "Gibson Business Park." Also in 1985, the plant expansion was completed bringing total AP capacity to 40 million pounds per year.

In November of 1985, AMPAC entered into an agreement to design, build, and lease a building for a manufacturer of food products (Kidd and Company marshmallows). During 1985, 55% of AP sales were for the Space Shuttle program. At the end of 1985, AMPAC had 139 employees.[12]

PEPCON Plant as depicted on the front of a piece of literature, Henderson, NV 1984

Impact of the January of 1986 Space Shuttle Challenger Accident

On January 28, 1986, the Space Shuttle Challenger failed on the launch sequence. This immediately put the program on hold indefinitely until a root cause could be determined (ultimately found to involve failed o-rings on the SRMs in very low launch temperature conditions). The event had a significantly negative impact on PEPCON because of the importance of this program to the sales of AP. AP sales for the Space Shuttle program were suspended for approximately 18 months. Thereafter, prior to the resumption of flights in 1988, PEPCON was directed to continue production of AP at a lower rate and to store AP at the PEPCON facility in Henderson as customer owned material in government owned aluminum bins until it was needed for resumption of Space Shuttle solid rocket motor production. Space Shuttle launches did not resume until later in 1988. During the period, the emergence of the Multiple Launch Rocket Systems (MLRSs) by the U.S. military resulted in increased sale of AP by PEPCON.

Other major customers of PEPCON from the early 1960s to the 1980s included Aerojet General Corp and Atlantic Research Corp. After the January of 1986 Shuttle Challenger accident, PEPCON increased AP sales to foreign customers located principally in Brazil and Europe.

In 1986, Space Shuttle related AP sales were 38% of total AP sales. Also in 1986, the Kidd and Company marshmallow plant adjacent to PEPCON was completed. This was the first occupant of the adjacent Gibson Business Park being developed by Ampac Development Company.[13]

In 1987, only 13% of AP sales were directed to the Space Shuttle program.[14]

PEPCON Plant and Adjacent Kidd and Company, 1987.

The Incident of May 4, 1988

On Wednesday, May 4, 1988, at just before noon local time, a large fire and a series of explosions completely destroyed the PEPCON plant, including the administrative offices and laboratories. This was a major event in the history of the company that resulted in the deaths of two employees, injuries to many other employees, tens of millions of dollars in damages, litigation involving scores of parties, and the eventual rebuilding of PEPCON's facilities from next to nothing. The event was captured by several persons using both still photography and videotape. The most important and dramatic record of the event was captured on videotape by Mr. Dennis Todd from atop Black Mountain (the Black Mountain videotape)—just two miles from the plant. The Black Mountain videotape images of the largest explosions were replayed on May 4 and the days thereafter by multiple national media outlets including CNN, CBS, NBC, and ABC News. The national interest in this event was driven by the combination of the unusual and dramatic videotape and the disruption of the supply of AP, which was of national importance due to its vital use in critical NASA and U.S. Department of Defense programs.

The general layout of the facility on May 4, 1988 is shown in Map 1.

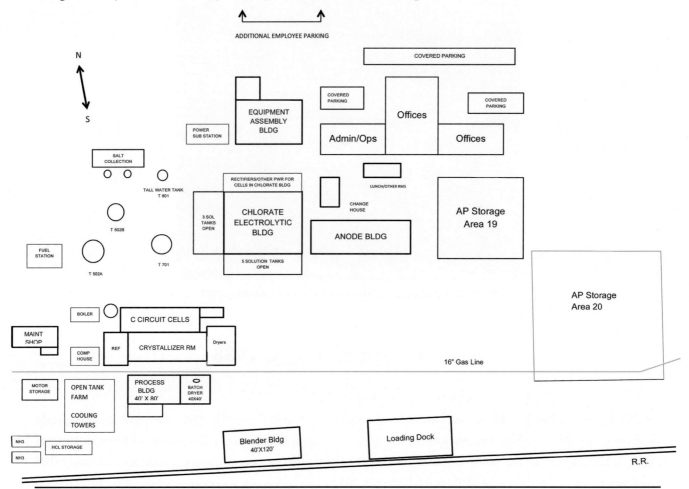

Map 1 – PEPCON Plant, Henderson, NV General Layout (1988)

November 2014

MAP 1

The Batch Dryer Room/Process building was a 40 feet wide by 120 feet long building. In the western 80 foot x 40 foot process section of this building, separated by a partition wall, ammonium chloride was stored until it was mixed with sodium perchlorate and then heated in six batch tanks to create AP. In the eastern 40 foot x 40 foot batch dryer room section of this building, the batch dryer was located, atop two large concrete supports, high enough to clear poly drums below for offloading, adjacent to the north wall with a Redler conveyor extending down at a roughly 45 degree angle to the floor where a Sweco was mounted. Typically, the batch dryer contained 10,000 pounds of AP.

The work taking place in this building included normal AP production tasks, for example, the blending of dry product to achieve desired particle size distributions. On this day, there was also repair work atop the west end of the Batch Dryer Room/Process building where two employees were using various tools, an acetylene cutting torch, and a welding rig on a catwalk to mend wind damage to the roof, which had occurred the previous weekend. Eyewitnesses verified that there was a fire watch (the second person was on the ground with a water hose wetting down areas where slag might fall from overhead) when the cutting torch was in use. There was also an excavating contractor who was digging a hole with a backhoe immediately to the west of the Batch Dryer Room/Process building in the same area as the roof repair. In addition, there were several employees (including Frank Quintana) and a supervisor (Larry Cummings) working on cleaning out large-solution storage tanks to the west of the building.

The fire began at approximately 11:45 a.m. in the Batch Dryer Room/Process building. Multiple eyewitnesses interviewed by PEPCON reported two distinct fires: one at the east end near the batch dryer and another in a drum on the west side of the partition wall near the south entrance to the building. When the fire was observed in the Batch Dryer Room, no one was inside. The initial in-plant radio report of the fire was made by Raymond Jackson, who was approximately 20 feet east of the building where he saw the fire through the east door. The Fire Department (reached via 911) was called at approximately 11:51 a.m.

Eyewitnesses reported that seven different employees began operating water hoses in an attempt to extinguish the two fires. Water from one fire hose was directed at the drum west of the partition wall by Bob Williams and then Jim Hamilton, which extinguished the blaze before the first explosion behind the batch dryer. One of the two employees repairing the roof at the west end of the building attempted to apply water from the elevated catwalk but with limited effect. Clyde Simon and then Frank Quintana used another fire hose to direct water through the east door of the building. There were seven other employees who observed the fire in this area first hand; the experienced employees among them reported that the response of the fire to the application of water seemed unusual compared to fires involving AP in the past, which were quickly extinguished with water.

The fire grew beyond its incipient stage, became very intense, and, because of the high winds out of the northeast, involved nearby AP storage and then the Batch Dryer Room/Process building to the north. Many employees began to evacuate the area at this point. Eyewitnesses reported that, approximately seven minutes after the fire started, and after attempts to extinguish the fire were made by plant personnel, there was an explosion outside of the building immediately to the north of the Batch Dryer Room. The explosion, which was strong enough to cause ceiling tiles in the administration building approximately 600 feet away to fall, increased the urgency of evacuating the plant site. There were many employees who acted quickly to make sure that coworkers were evacuated in a matter of minutes. These actions were essential in minimizing the number of fatalities and injuries. Eyewitnesses to the explosion reported that an aluminum bin containing approximately 4,400 pounds of AP was at the site of the explosions where a 16-inch natural gas line passed beneath the plant.

Subsequent to the first explosion near the batch dryer, the fire continued to grow in intensity and to spread to other parts of the plant site. There followed six clearly identifiable explosions (at least two were high order detonations and the rest were deflagrations). The explosion experts retained by PEPCON's insurer, Wilfred Baker Engineering and Failure Analysis Associates (now Exponent), and other experts determined that the last detonation—in Area 20 where PEPCON records indicated approximately 3.0 million pounds of AP was stored—had a TNT equivalency of approximately 1.5– 2.25 million pounds. In fact, the explosion registered 3.5 on the Richter scale at Cal Tech in southern California. The explosion experts based their scientific conclusions on evidence at the site, including the deformation of metal—a reliable indicator of explosion strength. The yield of the first explosion north of the batch dryer, which experts determined was not a detonation, in one aluminum bin holding approximately 4,400 pounds of AP, was estimated to be 38 pounds (17 kg) to 90 pounds (41 kg) TNT equivalent.[24] There were several other explosions, including two detonations on the loading dock east of the blender building and two detonations in storage Area 19 (south of the administration building).

The explosions also destroyed the nearby Kidd and Company marshmallow plant, which was located to the northwest of the PEPCON plant although, even during the fire's most intense moments, it did not extend to the Kidd and Company plant. Instead, as documented vividly by the Black Mountain videotape, a pressure wave ran from the PEPCON plant to the Kidd and Company plant. Nonetheless, Kidd and Company employees were able to evacuate and although there were injuries, there were no fatalities at its facility. Although the PEPCON plant was remote from dense populations, there was substantial damage to both commercial and residential dwellings in all directions. The Bonanza Materials gravel plant office approximately 2,000 feet to the west sustained substantial damage to its offices. Industrial facilities to the east also sustained some damage. The damage to residential dwellings, including broken glass windows, garage door damage, and some damage to concrete, was a result of over pressures.

There were 74 PEPCON employees (out of approximately 120) on site at the time the fire started. Although nearly all escaped with no injuries, tragically, there were two fatalities; both were long time employees: LeRoy (Roy) E. Westerfield, the controller, and Bruce Halker, the plant manager. Mr. Westerfield was in the administration building and summoned the fire department. (A recording of Mr. Westerfield's 911 call was replayed often in media reports). Mr. Westerfield did not evacuate the administration building and his remains were never found. The explosion in Area 19 was so intense that it leveled the entire administration building, which was followed by a larger explosion in Area 20.

Mr. Halker was in his office at the time the fire started. When the in-plant radio calls alerted those in the administration building of the fire, the assistant plant manager, Dave Thayer, stuck his head into Mr. Halker's office and told him the fire was large; both then ran together upwind of the administration building. Mr. Halker was later seen running through plant areas directing employees to evacuate. At the time of the first large explosion in Area 19, Mr. Halker had retreated to an area near his car at the administration building area. Meanwhile, Mr. Thayer had evacuated others including his father, Robert Thayer, to an area approximately 100 feet further away. Mr. Thayer yelled at Mr. Halker to move back but Mr. Halker did not appear to hear him. Just as Mr. Thayer was about to move closer to Mr. Halker, the Area 19 explosion occurred. Mr. Halker was not seen alive after that explosion; emergency crews found his remains when they entered the area hours after the last large explosions. Mr. Thayer and the 3-4 people with him, including his father, Robert Thayer, were picked up by the force of the Area 19 blast and thrown 50-100 feet across the parking lot at the north end of the plant. Several minutes later, the last and largest explosion in Area 20 drove this group beyond the edge of the parking lot into the evaporation pond. In fact, the force of this last explosion was enough to blow the coveralls off of Robert Thayer and deformed (dished in) the HP calculator in the shirt pocket of Dave Thayer.

The fire and explosions destroyed all of the plant buildings; in addition, 4 or 5 buildings at the west end of the plant, and thus upwind, sustained major structural, but not fire, damage. Approximately 40 cars in the employee parking lots were destroyed, vertical steel structures were deformed, and multiple rail cars at the adjacent railroad tracks to the south either were heavily deformed or were overturned by the force of explosions.

All of the on-site PEPCON records, including the contents of a "fire proof" safe in the administration building, were destroyed. This included: design drawings, operation records, safety committee meeting minutes, and other important documents. Given that this was 1988, much less information was stored or backed up in electronic format. Nonetheless, out of an abundance of caution, the company made a weekly back-up tape of key financial data generated on a Data General system and stored it off site in a bank in Henderson. The last back up occurred a few days before the fire and was used to generate the best information on inventories at the plant at the time of the incident.

Images of the incident were captured by several individuals. A series of four photographs were taken by Richard Askew from one half mile southeast of the plant on Nevada State Route 146, which captured the fire spreading and the evacuation of employees before the Area 19 detonation. A series of several photos were taken by a tourist from Chicago visiting the Kidd and Company marshmallow facility, which was also notable because the photographs showed the plant and smoke column opposite of the view revealed by the Black Mountain videotape and showed the Batch Dryer Room/Process Building fire spreading prior to the first explosion. Most important to the post-incident investigation, however, was the Black Mountain videotape. Mr. Todd was on the mountain performing maintenance on radio towers and it was his standard practice to videotape parts of that process. He noticed the fire after the first explosion and captured the rest of the incident on a tripod mounted 8mm video camera. His videotape was sold to NBC in California and others a few hours after the incident and was shown repeatedly on national news on the night of May 4, 1988, and a few days thereafter. PEPCON acquired a complete copy of the Black Mountain videotape some 30 days later.

The best information available indicates that the duration of the incident, from the start of the fire to the last detonation in Area 20 at the east end of the plant, was 15 minutes. With the last explosion in Area 20, large parts of the 16" natural gas line were uncovered exposing a large rupture at two points and allowing large volumes of natural gas (methane) to discharge and burn uncontrolled for approximately one hour. No attempt was made to extinguish this fire. Instead, the local gas utility company turned off the gas service feeding this line approximately 1 mile away from the plant thereby stopping the fire. After the fire, multiple craters were evident, the largest being approximately 4 feet deep, 20 feet wide and 250 feet long. Likewise, in Area 19 south of the administration building, there were several craters approximately 3 feet deep, 8 feet wide and 10-50 feet long.

Fred D. Gibson, Jr. was just returning to the plant from an off-site appointment when the fire was in its early stages. He immediately went into the administrative offices and plant area to assist in evacuating all employees. Mr. Gibson was at the east end of the plant near Gibson Road when the largest explosions occurred, which caused an injury to his head, eardrums, and knee. Soon after the Area 20 explosion, he encountered an emergency vehicle, which took him back up into the plant, prior to the arrival of the Clark

County or Henderson Fire Departments and while there were fires still burning and before the 16-inch gas line, which fed a huge torch-like fire, was shut off. Mr. Gibson's return was to assess the situation but most importantly to turn off valves on a large acid storage tank to stop a discharge caused by the force of the explosions.

Company records that were recovered from the offsite back up tape by August of 1988 revealed that 10.3 million pounds (4,678 metric tons) of dry AP was on site on May 4, 1988. This information was provided to all parties in August of 1988.[22] Originally the amount of AP was estimated to be between 3,900 and 4,500 metric tons.

In addition to assessing the strength of the explosions on May 4, 1988, Failure Analysis Associates investigated the general combustion and explosive properties of AP, the fire sequence, the metallurgical properties of components, including the 16-inch natural gas line that ran under the plant, and the permeability of the underground area at the plant. Failure Analysis Associates conducted dozens of full-scale fire tests using AP provided by PEPCON, including that in poly drums, as well as fiberglass siding panels and aluminum bins present at the PEPCON plant. Failure Analysis Associates attempted to induce explosions in conditions similar to those that existed at PEPCON on May 4, 1988, but came to the conclusion that the AP could not explode in the absence of a fuel such as methane (natural gas). [28]

A fire cause and origin expert (Dr. John Rockett) was also retained by PEPCON's insurers. Dr. Rockett constructed a timeline for actions in the area where the fire started and interviewed all witnesses in the area, many of them multiple times. Dr. Rockett was assisted further by PEPCON employees who had extensive experience with AP, which was of value in attempting to determine what occurred on May 4, 1988.

Immediately after the incident, the Clark County Fire Department (CCFD) took exclusive control of the site asserting that it believed there should be an arson investigation. The CCFD excluded parties from the plant site, including PEPCON employees for a period of almost 30 days, and, with Southwest Gas, removed evidence from the site without PEPCON's permission and in the absence of PEPCON employees. PEPCON personnel were allowed to enter PEPCON's own property only when escorted by the CCFD and only in very limited areas. A walk through of the entire site by PEPCON employees and its experts occurred as a result of a court order on May 17 and 18, 1988, but only after a significant amount of evidence had been removed by the CCFD and Southwest Gas.

There was interest in the role of the natural gas pipeline in the incident since methane is a fuel. PEPCON itself made observations (but did not perform destructive testing) of the remaining pipeline, including the pipeline in Area 20, and in other areas in May of 1988 before the damaged pipe was eventually removed by Southwest Gas. After the incident, two areas of the pipeline, approximately 200 feet apart, were exposed revealing a "fishmouth" failure in the pipeline with evidence of scalloping and side-trimmed edges. There were chevron marks on the edge surface of sections "B41-B45" of the pipe under Area 20 that were later used by Failure Analysis to make conclusions about the condition of key sections of the pipeline before and after the large explosions and their likely role in the incident.[28]

The Batch Dryer Room/Process Building was elevated at its north side from asphalt grade. After the incident, it was discovered that a large piece of the building's concrete foundation near this location had been blown away and had landed on top of the dryer. There was a depression in the asphalt area north of the dryer outside the building where an aluminum bin containing AP had been located prior to the first explosion. Afterward, at that location, vertical steel pipes that extended from ground level approximately four feet into the air were bent significantly inward toward the dryer. All of this supports the conclusion that an explosion occurred at this location.[24]

CCFD Press Release – July 14, 1988

On July 14, 1988, the CCFD issued a two page press release, "Factors Contributing to Fire Ignition, Spread and Detonation." The CCFD listed "*welders cutting in hazardous area with no fire watch, structural components consisting of highly combustible fiberglass reinforced plastic and a highly flammable and detonable material being stored, combustible poly drums, over 8000, high density storage practices, near and around buildings where previous fires occurred, housekeeping and weather.*" A press conference was held in Las Vegas where the CCFD Fire Chief Roy Parrish and Captain Robert James elaborated for the Las Vegas media. Chief Parrish stated that "natural gas played no role in the initial cause and origin of the fire." There was no formal CCFD report on the accident. Nor did the CCFD respond to a letter from PEPCON dated June 30, 1988, which faulted the CCFD for its use of "limited and outdated information" to reach "conclusions" that were "unreliable and suspect."[31]

U.S. Department of Labor, Division of Occupational Safety and Health (DOSH) Findings (1988)

The DOSH team conducted its own investigation where at least 10 employees were interviewed. This was memorialized in a late 1988 report.[30] The DOSH report was authored by Steven Luzik (Supv. Chemical Engineer, Industrial Safety Division) and stated that "*The author's investigation was limited by him not being able to observe and inspect the plant site immediately following the disaster. The Arson Division of the Clark County Fire Department maintained control over the site for several weeks. The DOSH and PEPCON investigation teams were not permitted entry into the facility until 13 days after the event. The first significant DOSH inspections did not occur until 33 days after the fire. At that time, the damaged areas had been displaced or removed from the site. Other important evidence, such as an unedited video tape of the fires and explosions taken by a contractor on top of a mountain, evaluation reports of the various pieces of evidence taken by the Fire Department, and results of gas line pressure testing were not made available to either DOSH or the author. As a result of this and the general devastation of the plant caused by the detonations, definitive conclusions as to the origin and initiation-mode of the fire were not possible. The conclusions, as related to the fire origin and initiation mode, nevertheless, represent the most likely mechanisms responsible for what was observed, and close examination and evaluation of all available information.*"

The report went on to state the following conclusions:

- *"The origin of the fire, at the PEPCON plant, is determined to be at either the southside of the west wall partition or the north wall of the batch dryer building. The initiation mode of the fire is undetermined. Smoking, sparking of electrical equipment, or frictionally ignited gas are among the probable ignition sources.*
- *The extremely rapid fire spread in the process building and subsequent growth to other buildings was primarily due to the high-combustible fiberglass-reinforced siding panels and close spacing of adjacent buildings. High winds blowing in the northeasterly direction were a contributing factor.*
- *Fire spread from the process buildings to the main storage areas was principally due to the wicking effect of the polyethylene drums filled with product, indiscriminately stored throughout the process areas, and to a minor extent, due to flying fire brands and debris from the first explosion.*
- *Six or seven detonations occurred solely in areas where aluminum econobins or steel drums were utilized to store the product of nominal 200 micron particle sizes. There was strong evidence of combustion around the base of the batch dryer section of the process building on the northeast, and south sides, beneath the gas and telephone vaults, and portions of the asphalt paving.*
- *There was also strong evidence of a natural gas fire, prior to the second explosion, at the northeast edge of the plant with a 6 ft. x 200 ft. narrow band of soft sand. The leading edge of this sand bar is located approximately 1,110 feet from the batch dryer building."*

AMPAC/PEPCON's Conclusions

PEPCON's experts, as well as the investigations by other parties including DOSH as noted above reached a different conclusion. The interviews that PEPCON and others conducted demonstrated there indeed was a fire watch (with water hose) and that the welders were too far away (80-100 feet from the first-observed flames) for a welding spark to have ignited something in the area where a fire was first reported. The independent testing by PEPCON's experts, as well as other independent testing, confirmed that AP is not highly flammable or easily ignited or detonated.

The evidence gathered by Failure Analysis Associates supported its finding that there was a natural gas leak in the 16-inch line, which was caused by the lack of welding in several areas on the pipe, that the natural gas from that leak escaped into the Batch Dryer Room/Process Building, that it there found an ignition source, and that, once ignited, the flaming natural gas spread to a drum that contained contaminated AP. The progression of the natural gas fire from there was due to the quantity of combustible materials, including AP, which fed the natural gas fire. Failure Analysis Associates concluded, after reviewing the evidence and conducting multiple burn tests with AP and all materials known to be on the PEPCON site, that the high order detonations only occurred because the burning natural gas from a leaking gas line came into contact with AP.[28] Dr. John Rockett also concluded that natural gas played a role in the fire initiation in large part because AP is an oxidizer and requires a fuel to burn; that fuel was the escaping natural gas from the pipeline, which ignited and then came in contact with combustible materials.

Area 20 AP Storage, Gas Line ("fishmouth" area), Looking West toward Batch Dryer, August, 1988.

That AP was not the cause of the fire but was instead ignited, along with other combustible material by the flaming natural gas is demonstrated further by the fact that, after the accident, there was a significant amount of AP on the ground, which was not consumed in the fire and explosions. Furthermore, in other areas where AP was stored in plastic drums, the plastic drums were ignited by the flaming natural gas, but once those plastic drums were consumed, the AP inside them did not burn but remained intact. More than 100,000 pounds of AP was recovered, stored on site, and then shipped in 1989 to the new AP production plant in Cedar City, Utah for reprocessing (also shipped to the new facility was high purity AP from the west end of the plant, which escaped any involvement in the incident, including three aluminum bins with approximately 5000 pounds each and approximately 300 poly drums with 550 pounds each).

AMPAC had property insurance coverage for buildings, machinery and equipment, inventory and business interruption by AIG Insurance Group. The claims related to plant, equipment, inventory and costs directly related to the accident were approximately $25.7 M which was paid by 1989.[17] AMPAC also had liability insurance with stated coverage of $1 million per occurrence, $2 million in the aggregate and a $2 million limit applicable to occurrences arising out of "products completed operations" as well as legal defense costs. There was litigation between PEPCON and the liability insurance company commencing in 1989 over the extent of its coverage. What was paid ultimately significantly exceeded the coverage limits.

New Facility Planned for Southern Utah to Be Built As Quickly As Possible

AP was a critical chemical for both space exploration and military use and therefore the U.S. Government held hearings in Washington D.C. and performed site visits in 1988 to better understand the situation. PEPCON committed to re-building the plant as quickly as possible. Within a few days of the May 4, 1988, incident, due to various factors, AMPAC management decided to inform Clark County, Nevada and then Nevada Governor Richard Bryan that AMPAC would not attempt to re-build the AP plant at the former PEPCON plant site in Henderson. At the time of the incident, the population in the vicinity had moved in much closer than when the plant was originally designed and built in the 1950s. The continuation of the development of the Business Park where the PEPCON plant was located, however, was planned.

Site locations for a new facility were assessed including in areas within Nevada. Ultimately, a site was chosen in Iron County adjacent to Cedar City, Utah, where there was an ability to locate the plant and build it quickly, which was a desire of the customers of PEPCON including the U.S. Government.

A new facility was designed, based primarily on the memory of several key employees since records were destroyed, within a few months. Bank financing took approximately 5-6 months to be completed. A term loan of $92,000,000 was obtained to finance the construction of the new plant, approximately 15 miles west of Cedar City, Utah. The groundbreaking for this facility occurred in November of 1988. The facility was designed to occupy approximately 217 acres within 4,800 acres acquired by AMPAC at the Iron County, Utah site. This new facility, comprised of 19 new buildings and 127,000 ft^2 of manufacturing, storage, and administration area space, was built and operating by July of 1989, 14 months after the May 4, 1988, accident.[16] That time frame was a significant challenge that was met through a partnership of AMPAC and the U.S. Government, principally NASA.

The approximate total amount of finished perchlorate products (sodium perchlorate not used as intermediate to make AP, AP and potassium perchlorate) made at PEPCON between 1958 and 1988 was 220 million pounds.

Primary Litigation and Settlement (1992)

As a result of the May 4, 1988, incident, litigation ensued among the parties that had an interest or involvement in operations at the plant, including AMPAC/PEPCON, its customers, Clark County, and others. The primary litigation concerned subrogation by insurance companies, which paid out claims to residential and commercial insureds in the area—including for home damage—where the amounts were in excess of $75 million. (*Aetna Casualty & Surety, et al. v. Pacific Engineering, et al* [17,18].) There were personal injury cases against PEPCON directly in excess of $2 million. In December of 1988, Southwest Gas Corporation sued

PEPCON and PEPCON counter sued. There were over 50 law firms involved in the litigation at one point or another.

The primary litigation was settled in 1992. The firms that were party to the settlement included AMPAC/PEPCON and Southwest Gas Corporation and the amount of settlement was over $70 million, which went to various parties including insurance companies and private parties. AMPAC paid $8.1 million and its (PEPCON's) liability insurance company paid $7.5M into the settlement.[18]

Restructuring and the New Perchlorate Manufacturing Facility

After the accident, the operating subsidiary (formerly PEPCON) of the parent company, AMPAC, responsible for AP production was formed and named PEPCON Production, Inc. and thereafter ultimately Western Electrochemical Company (WECCO), which operates the perchlorate chemicals manufacturing facility in Cedar City/Iron County, Utah as of September of 2015. The new plant was constructed in a relatively isolated area. Natural gas service to the WECCO plant is handled differently than at PEPCON, principally in the configuration where lines are above rather than below ground so that the lines can be monitored more closely.

After the new plant became operational in July of 1989, sales of perchlorates in fiscal year 1989 (ending September 30, 1989) were limited to two months but totaled $8.9 million with equipment sales of $3.2 million and real estate sales of $1.8 million.

Kidd & Company marshmallows rebuilt their facility at the same location after the accident. At a later date, its facility was relocated. As of mid-2015, the Clark County School District Facilities Service Center occupies the building formerly occupied by Kidd.

The area where the PEPCON plant was located has been developed to include a variety of businesses including Ocean Spray Cranberries, Inc. since 1994 and employing approximately 140, and Touro University of Nevada (both located on American Pacific Drive), which opened in 2004 and is a health science center serving the greater Las Vegas area through two colleges: The College of Osteopathic Medicine and the College of Health and Human Services. There are approximately 1,400 students attending this facility located on American Pacific Drive in Henderson as of September, 2015.

About the Authors:

John R. Gibson worked at PEPCON on a part time basis starting in 1956 and visited the plant periodically until May, 1988. He joined AMPAC as a Board member in 1988 and after a career of more than 25 years at US Steel/USX Corporation in California, became a full time employee in 1992 supervising construction of a sodium azide production facility at AMPAC's Utah operations adjacent to the perchlorate chemical plant. He became President and CEO of AMPAC in 1997 and remained in that capacity until January 2010, and on the board of AMPAC until January, 2014. He was not at PEPCON on May 4, 1988.

Dave A. Thayer first joined PEPCON in 1983 as a Plant Engineer and then Assistant Plant Manager. He was involved in the design and construction of the new WECCO plant which manufactures perchlorate chemicals in Utah soon after May 4, 1988 and has continued in operations of the facility, including the perchlorate manufacturing activity. Mr. Thayer was at PEPCON on May 4, 1988 for the entire event. He is currently President and General Manager of the AMPAC Utah Operations Facility which is comprised of WECCO and other divisions and subsidiaries of AMPAC.

Others: Other current and former employees of PEPCON were consulted in preparing this document including Fred D. Gibson Jr.

Bibliography

1. PEPCON Annual Report, 1969.
2. PEPCON Annual Report, 1971.
3. PEPCON Annual Report, 1974
4. PEPCON Annual Report, 1975.
5. PEPCON Annual Report, 1976.
6. PEPCON Annual Report, 1977.
7. PEPCON Annual Report, 1978.
8. PEPCON Annual Report, 1980.
9. AMPAC Annual Report, 1982.
10. AMPAC Annual Report, 1983.
11. AMPAC Annual Report, 1984.
12. AMPAC Annual Report, 1985.
13. AMPAC Annual Report, 1986.
14. AMPAC Annual Report, 1987.
15. AMPAC Annual Report, 1988.
16. AMPAC Annual Report, 1989
17. AMPAC Annual Report, 1991
18. AMPAC Annual Report, 1992.
19. AMPAC Statement to News Media, Las Vegas, NV, May 7, 1988.
20. PEPCON History, 5 pages, 1984.
21. Invoice - Jackson-Marcus Supply Company issued to the Nevada Natural Gas Company, February 10, 1956 (for pipe installed under the PEPCON plant, Henderson, NV)
22. Pacific Engineering and Production Company General Plant Layout, Drawing 0825, Reference 0825L, with AP storage data as recovered from PEPCON records, signed by James J. Peveler (Executive Vice President) and Dave A. Thayer (Assistant Manager of Operations).
23. Clark County Fire Department Release, July 14, 1988, "Factors Contributing to Fire Ignition, Spread and Detonation." – 2 pages.
24. Deposition of Quentin Baker, February 19-20, 1991, In Re May 4, 1988 Fire Litigation, District Court, Clark County, NV, Case A264974.
25. Failure Analysis Associates, Fire Spread at the PEPCON Site, May 4, 1988, rev 2.0, 11-30-90.
26. www.valleyautomall.com, description of the Valley Auto Mall located at or east of Gibson Road in Henderson, NV
27. www.oceanspray.com, information on Ocean Spray Cranberries, Inc.
28. "Blueprint for Disaster: Destruction in the Desert," Discovery Network International, Temple Street Productions, 2006.
29. PEPCON employee Interviews, 1988
30. U.S. Department of Labor, Bruceton Safety Technology Center, Industrial Safety Division, "Fire and Explosions Investigation Pacific Engineering and Production Company of Nevada, May 4, 1988." 1988.
31. Pacific Engineering and Production Company of Nevada letter addressed to the Clark County Fire Department (R. Parrish), June 30, 1988.
32. Cover Photo - PEPCON Plant, December 1985, Industrial Photographics Associates for AMPAC

Printed in the United States
By Bookmasters